MENTORING: LEADERSHIP TO LEGACY

ALMON GUNTER

HIGHLY ACCLAIMED SPEAKER, AUTHOR, & CONSULTANT

SPEED, STRENGTH, CONDITIONING & LIFE COACH

FOREWORD BY:

DAVID C. HODGES JR.

CHAIRMAN AND CEO OF HODGES MANAGEMENT GROUP

Mentoring: Leadership to Legacy

For information or to request authorization to make copies of any part of this work contact:

AGE 3, LLC
Post Office Box 194
Jacksonville, Florida 32234
Office Phone 904.803.1917
Web Address: www.almongunterexperience.com
Email: almon@almongunterexperience.com

Twitter: @almongunter
Facebook: Almon Gunter Experience
LinkedIn: Almon Gunter
Instagram: Almon Gunter Experience
YouTube: Almon Gunter Experience
Podcast: Almon Gunter Experience
TikTok: @almongunterexperience

DEDICATION

This book is dedicated to all of the wonderful mentors I have had and have in my life over the years. Each of these mentors have played a major role in shaping my life spiritually, personally, academically, athletically, socially, and professionally. I dedicate this book to them as a continuation of their leadership and legacy.

CONTENTS

FOREWORD

What an honor to be asked by Almon Gunter to write the foreword for this book, Mentoring: Leadership to Legacy. As you will discover in reading this book, Almon has immense passion for pouring into others, specifically young student athletes. And as the father of one of his student athletes, I can tell you firsthand the profound impact he has in the lives of those he coaches and mentors.

Reading this book will give you a sense of his passion, but in my humble opinion does not replace the real thing, which is dynamic and special beyond what you could expect. There are not many more upbeat positive people than "Coach". He chooses not to have bad days. And his upbeat positive nature is infectious. But don't allow the positivity to trick you into thinking he is just sunshine and rainbows. Quite the contrary, he is always motivating, pushing, challenging, and demanding excellence from everyone around him.

COACH HAS WRITTEN A WONDERFUL GUIDEBOOK WITH MENTORING: LEADERSHIP TO LEGACY. HE OPENS UP HIS PAST ON ALL THOSE WHO HAVE IMPACTED HIS LIFE AND GIVES A SNAPSHOT INTO THE LITERALLY HUNDREDS OF STUDENT ATHLETES HE IS EITHER CURRENTLY MENTORING OR HAS MENTORED. YOU WILL BE ENCOURAGED BY THE LEGACY HIS GRANDPARENTS HAVE LEFT IN HIM. AND COACH IS PAYING IT FORWARD BY LEAVING THOSE LESSONS HE LEARNED AND SO MANY MORE, IN YOUNG PEOPLE (AND OLD ONES LIKE ME) EACH AND EVERY DAY.

I KNOW YOU WILL BE BLESSED AND ENCOURAGED BY READING THIS BOOK. AND I HOPE YOU WILL BE CHALLENGED AS I HAVE BEEN, TO FIND A MENTOR, BE A MENTOR, AND LEAVE A LEGACY.

DAVID C. HODGES JR. —CHAIRMAN AND CEO OF HODGES MANAGEMENT GROUP

INTRODUCTION

"EDUCATION IS A PASSPORT TO THE FUTURE, FOR TOMORROW BELONGS TO THOSE WHO PREPARE FOR IT TODAY." MALCOLM X

When I read this quote by Malcolm X what immediately comes to mind is that the game of life is about the information you receive, the decisions you make with that information, and in what timeframe you use it. No matter where you want to be in your life, education can put you there. Malcolm X is one of the greatest examples of what is possible when you understand, focus, commit, and hold yourself accountable to being an advocate for your life through formal and informal education. He is a great example of the saying, "it's not where you start in life, it's where you finish." By betting on himself Malcolm X went from a convicted felon, to one of the greatest leaders and advocates for civil and human rights in the world. Through the power of education, preparation, and effort he built bridges that many of us are still crossing over today.

As I look back over my life, I realize that I had and have some incredible mentors academically, athletically, spiritually, personally and professionally. Today more than ever I realize what I was given in the way of spiritually, personally and professionally. Today more than ever I realize what I was given in the way of leadership, self-advocacy and mentorship is priceless. There is no dollar amount or value I can put on the time that was given to me by others that has shaped my life. I was surrounded by a village of people who every day poured information into me that would give me the opportunity to not only compete in the game of life, but this information has allowed me to win the game every day. They dug a foundation within my soul that sat firmly on the bedrock of faith, courage, respect, attitude and effort. Through their examples of servant leadership and bridge building I am who I am today. I am truly one that the village raised.

If you've read any of my previous books before you know I describe myself as a nerd. But when you combine a nerd with physical world class athletic abilities you actually end up with a super hero. When you explore super heroes' backgrounds what you usually find are brilliant people who somehow have super human strength in some capacity mentally or physically or both, and they use it to benefit humanity. The difference in the hero and villain in many cases always comes down to character. It comes down to doing what's right for the masses versus doing what's right for one or two people. The villain often thinks in terms of me, mine, and I, whereas the hero thinks in terms of us, we, and ours. The hero simply understands that no one wins alone. We all need help to succeed.

I can remember my grandfather (Wilson Gunter) saying, "son if you have trouble finding a role model, the library is full of them." Fortunately for me finding role models was easy. My mother, father, stepfather, and grandfather were always leading the way with their actions, as well as their words. And my neighborhood was flooded with people who were amazing leaders and mentors. As far as role models go my paternal grandfather (Wilson Gunter) was king. He was and still is the smartest person I've ever known. He had a 6th grade education formally, but had a PHD in the greatest game of all life! He was 5 feet 4 inches tall about 130 pounds (that's being very generous regarding height and weight) of hard working, principle driven, no nonsense badass. He led with his life every day. And if my grandfather was the king of leadership, mentors and role models my mother (Eunice Gunter) was indeed the queen. She was the poster child for servant leadership. No one lead and served more people in one lifetime than my mother. Mom was as tough as they got but with a loving heart. There are so many lessons that she taught me throughout her lifetime and beyond. The following are some of my favorites:

1. She only said things once when she was giving instruction. If she had to say it more than once it wasn't going to be good for anyone. This rule taught me how to be a good listener.

2. Mom would say, "Wherever you cut up, I'm going to cut up. You cut up in school, I'm going to cut up in school. You cut up in the store. I'm going to cut up in the store." There was none of that wait until we get home crap. This rule taught me how to be respectful and responsible.

3. Mom would also say, "It doesn't cost anything to be kind. You never know who may need to hand you a glass of water." This rule taught me to treat people the way I wanted to be treated.

4. She encouraged me to write myself a love letter periodically. "Know your value as a person always." She would say. This rule taught me to know my value and be responsible for my happiness.

5. Mom would say, "Some of the bridges you build are not for you to cross. They are for others to cross. Build the bridge anyway." Be a bridge builder. This rule taught me not to be selfish. Make things better even if I weren't going to directly benefit from it.

School was a place that I truly loved being. Within those walls I always felt that whatever questions I had about anything, I could find the answers there. I learned early on that in school that I got to decide how much I wanted to learn and exactly what I wanted to learn. I can still remember the names of every teacher I had from elementary school until my high school graduation. I can also remember the names of every adult person who lived on the street that I lived on (Delmonte Street). Heck, actually I know the names of all the adults in my neighborhood. Every one of those teachers and members of my neighborhood had an impact on me in one way or another. College was more of the same when it came to the willingness to learn. I worked hard to connect with as many of my professors as I could because I refused to be just another face in the crowd. I can't say I remember all of my professors by name but I can definitely say I can remember most of them. Especially the professors that challenged me, pushed me, and help me to grow in ways that I didn't know was possible.

In college being a student athlete was very challenging because of the demands academically and athletically. 14 hours days every day with no end in sight can make you question yourself about everything. It was in these moments that the years of having strong leaders and mentors in my life really paid off. All of the things that I had been taught about persistence, patience, commitment and sacrifice came shining through. The ability to keep getting up that one more time than I was knocked down was a direct result of me always being willing to learn, listen, and grow no matter the situation.

Having a strong support system to lean on made all of the difference in the world. When you know that there are people cheering for you, praying for you and who love you unconditionally there is no ceiling, there is no limit.

Just as each teacher in my academic career brought something unique to my life, so did each person in the village that raised me. Reading history is one thing, but getting the story from people who lived it is an entirely different thing. It was the stories that were told by my great grandmother, grandparents, mother, father, aunts, uncles, and their friends that inspired me to learn, risk, and grow each day. The stories prepared me in ways that books could not. How could I be afraid to fail, or fall, or play small, when so many people before me gave their life in order for me to have the right to life, liberty, and the pursuant of happiness? It was the village that allowed me to have courage. Courage to dream big, courage to grow big, courage to do big, and courage to live big.

I am forever grateful for the many mentors I have had and have in my life. Without mentors I am not sure where my path would have led me. Leaders who make the decision to serve and mentor others understand the assignment that we all have been given. And that assignment is an assignment of service to others. Servant leadership is the cornerstone to building a legacy that last for generations. As my mother would say, "You can do bad by yourself baby, but you can't win by yourself." Every success in our life has come as a result of someone's help. Whether we choose to acknowledge it or not, someone helped us to succeed. Leaders who are open to sharing what they know with others not only can change their mentee's life, but often times change their own life. I often say to people the information that I share isn't mine, it's a gift that was given to me to pass on. Legacies are created through information and action. Information is the true revolution because it can inspire individuals to risk and grow in ways that no other one thing can.

My grandfather inspired me not by his words, but by how his actions aligned with what he said daily. For him every day was an opportunity to be better, to get closer to achieving your dreams, to serve others with your actions not words. As for my mother, even to this day she is the inspiration for everything I do. As she would say, "Just find one reason every day to be better." Mom kept things simple always. She taught me that 20 seconds of courage was all that was needed to breakthrough any situation and succeed.

As you read the following pages, as always, read with an open heart and open mind. Look within yourself because success is always an inside job. My sincere hope is that within this book you will find the information to be both inspiring and motivating so you can compete and play the most important game of all, life, at your highest level. Enjoy another journey as we once again ride together on the A-Train!

CHAPTER 1

What is Mentoring

Mentoring. *My definition of mentoring is: to serve as a model, a counselor, an advisor, coach, and a tutor for a person or persons. Mentoring is a relationship in which an experienced or more knowledgeable person helps to guide a less experienced or less knowledgeable person. The mentor provides support, guidance, and advice to the mentee, helping them to develop their skills, knowledge, and confidence. It is a valuable way for people to learn from those who have more experience and to benefit from their insights and wisdom.*

Mentoring can be especially valuable for people who are just starting out in their careers, as it can help them navigate the challenges and opportunities that they may face. It can also be beneficial for those who are looking to make a career change, as a mentor can provide valuable guidance and support as they learn new skills and adjust to their new roles. Additionally, mentoring can be a way for people to build their personal and professional network, as it allows them to form relationships with others in their field.

Mentoring is a great way for an individual, to produce someone greater than oneself. As a leader your mentee or successor should always be more than you are. A leader is the foundation and a true mentee or successor never destroys the foundation, it builds upon it. Being a mentor is a great way to ensure the knowledge you've gained and the things you have built throughout your lifetime live on. As a mentor you are intentionally transferring knowledge, insight, and wisdom through practical experiences and relationships to the mentee in hopes for their continued growth. Mentors serve always.

Mentoring is often confused with coaching. It is true that mentoring and coaching are both needed for growth in an individual however, there are some differences between the two. (The best mentors always bring an element of coaching into their mentoring sessions.) I will start with the key components of **Mentoring**:

- To be a mentor, no qualifications are needed. Mentorship is based on one's knowledge, wisdom, and experiences over time. It's the ability to transfer knowledge, insight, and experience to another for their continued growth and development.
- Mentoring is often more of a long-term arrangement. Mentorships can last for weeks, months, or years.

Some mentorship can last a lifetime. A mentor who has been a true blessing in my life personally and professionally for over 20 years is Pat Williams, Hall of Fame and Sr Vice-President of the Orlando Magic. Over 20 plus years ago Pat took me under his wings and guided me on how to be a servant leader, dynamic speaker, and entrepreneur. It was Pat who encouraged me to write my first book Focus on The Final Seconds and Win the Game of Life nearly 20 years ago. Even today he is still helping me stay my course.

- There is no real structure for mentoring. The mentor and mentee usually decide how they what the relationship to go. Usually there isn't a set agenda however, setting an agenda or creating goals are up to the mentor and mentee.
- Mentorship at its' core is about development. It is up to the mentee to decide the things they want to learn and develop.

Key components of **Coaching**:
- Coaching encourages individuals to perform and execute day in and day out. It's usually more performance driven.
- Coaching is more non-directive unlike mentoring. It's

about posing the right questions, empowering and trusting individuals who are being coached to figure out how they can achieve more.

- There are training skills and qualifications to being a coach. And to coach you almost always need some type of certification or meet some qualifications to coach others.
- Most coaching situations in business organizations are short-term. Athletic coaching can be long term as far as having the same coach however, the people being coached can change year to year or day to day.
- In coaching the people who are being coached are usually selected by the coach, administration, or organization.

Just as there are key differences between mentoring and coaching there are key skills required between the two. To be a mentor even though there are no qualifications you certainly must have a desire to help others. You must have knowledge and insight in the area that the mentee is interested and be willing to be available long-term to develop the mentee. And finally, you must be willing to inspire, motivate, and encourage the mentee to do the things necessary to achieve their goal.

The skills to be an effective coach requires a mutual understanding and respect between the coach and the person that is being coached and the ability to maximize resources and inspire the person being coached. As a coach you must have the ability to recognize the strengths and challenges of the person who is being coached and teach them the skills needed to tackle problems head on and not dwell on the situation. And finally, a coach finds a way to connect interpersonal skills and practical skills to convert discussions into actions.

The following side-by-side comparison gives a great snapshot of the differences between coaching and mentoring.

Topic	Coaching	Mentoring
Timeframe	Relationship is more likely to be *short-term* (up to 6 months or 1 year) with a specific outcome in mind. However, some coaching relationships can last longer, depending on goals achieved.	Relationship tends to be more *long-term*, lasting a year or two, and even longer.

Focus	Coaching is more *performance driven,* designed to improve the professional's on-the-job performance.	Mentoring is more *development driven,* looking not just at the professional's current job function but beyond, taking a more holistic approach to career development.
Structure	Traditionally more *structured,* with regularly scheduled meetings, like weekly, bi-weekly or monthly.	Generally, meetings tend to be more *informal,* on an as needed basis required by the mentee.
Expertise	Coaches are hired for their expertise in a given area, one in which the person who is being coached desires improvement. Examples: Presentation skills, leadership, interpersonal communication, sales.	Within organization mentoring programs, mentors have more seniority and expertise in a specific area than mentees. The mentee learns from and is inspired by the

		mentor's experience.
Agenda	The coaching agenda is co-created by the coach and the person who is being coached in order to meet the specific needs of the that person.	The mentoring agenda is set by the mentee. The mentor supports that agenda.
Questioning	Asking thought-provoking questions is a top tool of the coach, which helps the person who is being coached make important decisions, recognize behavioral changes and take action.	In the mentoring relationship, the mentee is more likely to ask more questions, tapping into the mentor's expertise.
Outcome	Outcome from a coaching agreement is specific and measurable, showing signs of improvement or positive change in the desired performance area.	Outcome from a mentoring relationship can shift and change over time. There is less interest in specific, measurable results or changed behavior

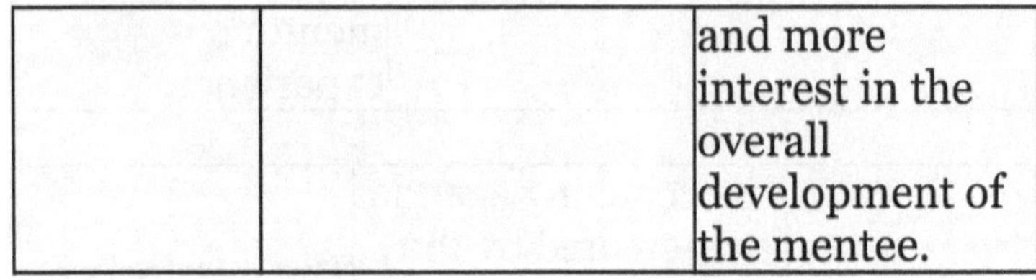

		and more interest in the overall development of the mentee.

Mentoring and coaching both have incredible benefits. They both are highly effective learning tools, both can increase retention in organizations and development of individuals, both are easy to implement, and both can improve individual performance. But it's important to know when a mentor should be used verses when a coach should be used. The following are tips on when to use a mentor:

1. Motivate a talented person to focus on their career or life development.
2. Inspire individuals to see what is possible in their life or career.
3. Enhance a person's personal or professional leadership development.
4. Transfer knowledge from one person to another.
5. For succession or legacy planning.

Why does mentoring matter? Mentoring matters because it can have a significant impact on an individual's personal and professional development. A mentor can provide valuable guidance, support, and encouragement as a mentee grows and learns. This can help to build confidence and self-esteem, and can also serve as a source of motivation and inspiration.

Mentoring also matters because it can help bridge the gap between different generations and levels of experience. It can allow those who are just starting out, and it can also provide an opportunity for those who are less experienced to learn from and be guided by those who have more knowledge and expertise. This can create a sense of community and connection within an organization or industry, and can also help to foster collaboration and teamwork. Overall, mentoring can be a powerful tool for personal and professional development, and can have a lasting impact on an individual personally and professionally.

The following are two personal stories about how a few incredible mentors shaped my life.

Story number one.

In 1991 I was working for American Transtech an AT&T Company. I started out working on the phone but soon after was promoted to being an instructor. Donna Williams was my supervisor and she was an incredible leader. Working for her taught me a great deal. However, there was this guy I would see every day walking through the atrium, very distinct, always dressed sharp, and he was a big man in statue. I found out his name was Richard Valentine. Later I found out he was Ms. William's husband and I introduced myself to Mr. Valentine. Mr. Valentine was an executive for AT&T and he happened to be African-American. I asked him to lunch and well I had questions. And as luck would have it, Mr. Valentine had answers! I asked him to mentor me and without hesitation he said he would. When I found out his background I was blown away. He was one of the first four African-Americans to play football for Virginia Military Institute (VMI). He told me how it shaped his life and helped him to learn how to work through hard stuff. He helped me to understand what it took to grow into a leader and what sacrifices that needed to be made to achieve my goals. This was all transferrable knowledge because at the same time I was training and competing as a world-class track athlete. One piece of advice he gave me was to stay away from negative people. Mr. Valentine said when you enter this building always move with a purpose. He told me to buy a briefcase and he didn't care what I put in it, but walk in with that briefcase every day and walk like I had somewhere to be. I bought a briefcase that same afternoon. He said when negative people got near, just grab that briefcase and say, "I would love to talk with you but I have somewhere to be." That was a very valuable lesson for me. I still have that briefcase today. Mr. Valentine helped me to developed the skills I needed to be promoted over and over again until I become a very young executive for AT&T Universal Card and beyond. He never stopped being a great mentor and guiding light in my life.

Story number two.

In 2001 I met Dr. David B Langston in Tampa Florida. We were both invited to attended a party for a professor at the University of South Florida. We were staying in the same hotel and somehow when it was time to head over to the party, we met walking to our cars and Doc ended up riding to the party with me. We talked for hours and never really mingled at the party. We had a lot in common. Both countries boys, both grandfathers were our heroes, and both wanted to help kids. Doc told me about a foundation he had started Norris B Langston Youth Foundation. His brother was killed in an industrial accident so he started a foundation in his honor. Doc played basketball at Drake University and then professionally with Philadelphia. He went on to get his PHD. Doc was a badass. The guy had grit and determination that was next level. His mom died when he was 4 years old and his father died his very first day of college. He was told when he attended Drake that he would never graduate and I quote, "because he was black and from the south." Well, Doc took 21 credit hours per semester was a flat-out baller and graduated from Drake in record time. He told me about his foundation and I told him about being a speaker and working with student athletes and Doc said I have a program in 3 weeks at North Florida Community College in Madison Florida would you come speak. I said of course. Now that guy had just met me, but here he was betting on me. Betting that I could do would I say I could. I went to the program, spoke first and never spoke first at our program again. Doc said man you are the closer. No one wants to follow you! Doc took me under his wings and taught me how to lead but more importantly how to give back. He poured so much into me and then introduced me to the guy who would become my spiritual advisor, colleague, mentor, and brother Dennis Webber (DDub). The 3 of us would travel the state of Florida for the next 8 years until Doc passed away in March of 2009. DDub and I would continue the mission of inspiring kids together until he passed away in October of 2020. I remember every lesson that Doc and DDub taught me. These guys were solid as a rock. Always standing in the gap to help kids be the best versions of themselves. There is not a day that goes by that I don't lean on something they did or said.

The legacy of Ms. Donna Williams, Mr. Richard Valentine, Dr. David B Langston, and Dr. Dennis W Webber will live on, because it lives within me. I have shared their stories and ideas for years and will continue to do so throughout my life. The servant leader knows that mentoring matters. They know the importance of having something that outlives themselves. As a leader the greatest gift you can give, is the gift of mentorship.

Scribbles and Doodles

Do you have a mentor? (If so, what is your overall focus with your mentor? If not, what are you waiting on?)

____

____

____

____

____

____

____

____

____

____

Do you have a mentee? (If so, what is your overall focus with your mentee? If not, what are you waiting on?)

____

____

____

____

____

____

____

____

____

____

List 3 things you want to accomplish with your mentor. List 3 things you want to accomplish with your mentee.

____

____

____

____

____

____

____

____

____

Final Thoughts:

____

____

____

____

____

____

____

____

____

CHAPTER 2

The Purpose of Mentoring

The purpose of mentoring is to provide support, guidance, and advice to a less experienced or less knowledgeable individual, with the goal of helping them to develop their skills, knowledge, and confidence. One of the main purposes of mentoring is to support personal and professional development. A mentor can help a mentee to identify and pursue their goals, and can provide guidance and support as they work to achieve those goals. This can include helping the mentee to develop new skills, improve their performance, and advance their career. Additionally, a mentor can provide encouragement and inspiration, and can help the mentee to build confidence and self-esteem.

Another purpose of mentoring is to foster learning and growth. A mentor can provide valuable insights and knowledge, and can help the mentee to gain a deeper understanding of their field or industry. This can be especially valuable for those who are just starting out in their careers, or for those who are looking to make a career change. A mentor can also provide guidance on how to navigate the challenges and opportunities that may arise as the mentee pursues their goals. Overall, the purpose of mentoring is to support the personal and professional development of the mentee, and to help them to grow and learn as they pursue their goals.

You cannot have mentorship without leadership. Leadership is something the world needs and without it many things will not and cannot happen. Without leadership nothing happens, nothing improves, nothing develops, nothing begins, nothing succeeds, nothing progresses and nothing changes. It is the first step in creating something that will last beyond the original founder.

As a leader the areas of mentoring and coaching should be focal points to ensuring a successful succession plan. However, many times these 2 areas are often the weakest for leaders to master. Mentoring and coaching often get confusing for leaders because even though they are similar in nature they have some key differences. And it's these differences that can cause leaders to come up short when preparing the next group of leaders. Producing other great leaders should not be left up to chance, it should always be done with intentionality and purpose. Mentoring is a proven way to go from leadership to legacy.

The leadership role is critical for the success of any organization. It doesn't matter if we are talking professional organizations, non-profit organizations, sports organizations, civic organizations, or families, leadership matters. Leadership provides the vision, the initiative, passion, and energy to inspire others to a specific goal to benefit all. The ability as a leader to make all of these things happen for every person involved is no easy task, but successful leaders work diligently to make it happen. One of the keys to making sure as a leader you are hitting the mark in these areas is to develop your people skills. People skills help you to make the critical connections needed when sharing your vision with others. People skills is often defined as the ability to listen, to communicate, and to relate to others on a personal or professional level. People skills can also include the ability to work with others toward achieving a common goal, the ability to show empathy, and having the ability to find solutions to problems.

Having a vision is a huge first step but you must be able to communicate your vision in such a way that others are eager to follow. Getting buy-in from the people you are leading goes a long way in the success of the vision. As a leader you have to lead with your life always. Communicating the right message at the right time is a good thing, but if the actions of the leader doesn't compliment the words others will quickly select themselves out of the mission. A leader's passion and energy matters if he or she is going to move individuals from the known to the unknown. You must be able to sell the vision and make the future more important to the people than the present.

The real greatness in leadership doesn't come from building buildings. The real greatness in leadership comes from building people. The greatest act of leadership, is the act of mentoring. Providing knowledge that inspires individuals to learn, risk and grow beyond what he or she can immediately see is legacy. One of the greatest accomplishments of any leader is the accomplishment of succession. It' s leaving a person and plan in place that will continue to grow beyond the leader. As a leader when you fail to mentor a successor you are cancelling your leadership legacy. The only way any of us can live on is through people. As a leader if your vision does not live on beyond you, you fail.

As a leader when you think about succession it is important to understand that succession is never about you. It's about the next generation. The goal of any succession plan should always be to focus on preserving success. As a leader your purpose can only stay alive through succession. Succession is the perpetuation of purpose and we all should strive to find and live out our purpose. Leaders who focus on succession realize that succession is a transfer of confidence from the leader to the successor, as well as the leader's purpose, passion, intent, vison, standards, values, character, morals, and qualities to the next generation of leaders.

The legacy of leadership is made possible through mentorship. Being a mentor is how success at any level continues to thrive for generations to come. The simplest explanation surrounding the purpose of why being a mentor matters is legacy. It is the continuation to live long after you are gone. Mentorship says you understood the assignment of being a servant of people, a catalyst for conflict, challenge, and change, and more importantly a builder of men and women.

Without a doubt the greatest mentor I have ever had was my paternal grandfather Wilson Gunter. It was he, that instilled in me the desire to want to be all that I could be. It was my papa who helped me to understand that the saying you only live once is inaccurate, because the truth of the matter is you have the opportunity to live each and every day. Through my papa I realized that living 2000 years was not only possible but doable if you focused on being a builder of men and women. Helping people to build a foundation of core principles and values that could hold anything you placed on top of them is the essence of leadership.

My papa was born on September 11, 1906 and when I do the math, he is still living 116 years later because his stories and lessons are still being told by me and other family members. He captured my attention with his words, but he inspired me through his actions. My papa not only told me the way, but he showed me the way every day, His knowledge was incredible and his wisdom priceless. In a world that constantly tried to convince him that he was less than my papa bet on himself and wrote his on story.

His succession plan was simple. It was to empty his cup of all that he had experienced and learned throughout his years to anyone that was open to the possibilities of life. My papa never held back knowledge. He gave all that he had. But like any great leader or mentor he never set out to be such a great leader or mentor, it happened because his life's work spoke for itself. So, like myself, many people came to him and followed his lead, soaked up his wisdom, and therefore continued to grow his legacy.

For a legacy to last forever, it requires that you are intentional in your pursuit of mentorship and leadership. Like all things in life that are worth having, you have to work at it. I worked hard at being the kind of mentee that my papa could build into a great person. I was obsessed with learning from him so I could build on what he had started. It was important to me to continue his work of leadership and service to ensure that the next generation would know that we are a combination of all the generations before us. There was a price paid by generations before us that gave us all of the opportunities we have today.

So, my children and my children's children all hear the stories of my papa and my paternal great grandfather Dan Gunter and paternal great grandmother Julia Hunt and my maternal grandfather Levi Shannon and grandmother Ronita Shannon, how they paved the way for where we are now. I am intentional in my delivery to my children on why mentorship, leadership, and legacy are so important. However, I don't just share these stories with family, as a coach, speaker, author, and mentor to hundreds of thousands of people over the past 25 years, the lessons, knowledge, and wisdom that my papa and mother shared with me I have shared with all that would listen. If you ask anyone who has spent more than 5 minutes with me in conversation, chances are a quote or story from my papa or mother has probably come up. Every generation should know that they have a purpose, they have value, and they have a gift or gifts that the world truly needs. We need mentorship if we are going to live beyond our life. Leadership without a successor or succession plan is failure.

Mentorship serves as the cornerstone to building a legacy that last many generations beyond yourself. Just as we strive to create generational wealth financially, I think it is more important to create generational wealth emotionally, spiritually, as well, leave a legacy of strong character, knowledge and wisdom. For me these are the gifts that keep on giving.

A story of purpose:

Sometimes the thing we are supposed to do is right in front of us. Like most people I wanted to know my purpose. I think as a kid we all get sidetracked by thinking our purpose is somehow linked to our job, money, and things. The truth of the matter is we all get to define our own success. We all are the authors of our own life story. I have come to realize that when you find your work in life, you have just found your purpose in life. Your work simply is what you are born to do. It is your gift to share and only you can share it the way it was meant to be shared. I have had many successes but most of those successes were not my work. My mother knew my work and she helped me to find it, embrace it, pursue it, and do it. I never for once thought that helping kids to know their value, find their voice, and get 1% better each day would be my work, but here we are and it's without a doubt what I was born to do. The interesting thing is if I really stop and think about it, it was always the thing that brought me the most joy growing up. Helping people to get better, watching people succeed, winning as a team, these are the things that brought me the most joy. I often say I haven't had a job in 25 years which is true, but I have had my work.

Jenna Silverburg was the first student athlete I worked with and now I train her 11 years old daughter, which means coach is getting old. Every time I see Jenna's dad Dave, I blame him for getting me into the coaching mentoring business. But the truth of the matter is that it says a lot when the student athletes I've trained over the years bring their kids back to train with me, call for advice, and catch me up on their lives.

Former student athletes like McCall Zerboni who is still playing professional soccer for NJ/NY Gotham FC, it has been an absolute joy to watch her grow into an amazing woman. She is leading, mentoring, and developing others which makes me so proud of her for finding her work. I recently had dinner with McCall in NY and as we always do, we had an amazing time catching up. She reminded me of our first training sessions together over 13 years ago and how those first few sessions shaped her life. McCall is a special young lady. She has grit, tenacity, perseverance and there is just no quit in her. She makes it easy to cheer for her.

Athletes like Derrick Henry who is a beast on and off the football field, Ben Gamel and Jacob Young both professional baseball players and both still hunting every day to be better are why I say I haven't had a job in 25 years. They make my work fun. Avery Patterson (AP) who has totally revived UNC Chapel Hill women soccer program on and off the field. Student athletes like Michael Kelly, Naila Owens, Ashley Hurley, Brandt and Nick Duncan, Erin and Kristin Hoover, Gio Beachamp, Mikaela and Reef McGee are all crushing this game of life. My student athletes understand the assignment of sports have a shelf-life, you will become an RP (Regular Person) so know your value and live your purpose. When I think of all of the great student athletes that I was blessed to work with I sometimes get overwhelmed with joy: Charlotte Summerall, Danielle Gordon, the original redheads Angeline and Gabrielle Daly, Trey Sneed, the Robinson brothers, Josiah, Jaylon, and Jhoel, CJ and Brandon, Tremble, Jaden Canady, Kirk Reed Jr, Charlie Medure, Taya Edwards, Leah Ferlin, Brady Stringer, JP Mauriello who just became a MD, the Ohare's Andy, Morgan, Brooke, the Triglia's Bobby, Mikey and Caroline, all of my student athletes are champions because they win or learn, they never lose. They battle back from adversity and overcome setbacks that would crush the average person, but nothing about my student athletes is average.

Clayton Hodges (The Project), remember the name because this kid has been through it and came out the other side swinging. Not sure what is in store for him down the road, but I think it's something huge. 2 brain surgeries later and The Project is still showing up and fighting through the adversity to be great. I constantly push him, yet encourage him to leave no doubt about who he is and what type of person he is. Character matters, effort matters, leadership matters, that is the message I drill into him every day. Success comes with a price and you have to pay it every day. You can't rest on yesterday's laurels. I am definitely betting on The Project.

Christian Ventouras (aka Snacks) what an amazing story this student athlete is writing. He came to me in 2014 as a kid who just wanted to get in better shape. From there he transformed himself into an incredible offensive and defensive lineman in football. With scholarships on the table, he decided he would rather just focus on getting an engineering degree in college and not play football. However, Snacks continued to train with me all throughout his college career with me and completely transformed his body by losing 80 pounds. Then as the student athlete he is, he started competing in Spartan races. He simply transferred all the things that made him great on the football field to the rest of his life. He recently just graduated in May of 2023 with a degree in engineering and moved to Cincinnati Ohio for his first grown-up job. So proud of this kid. And before he headed to Cincy he reminded me that our time training together wasn't over. He is truly a champion.

Lane Fouraker (Diesel) underestimated by many his entire life, but will out work anybody, anytime, anywhere, not to mention his little sister Macie is an absolute go getter in everything she does. I am betting money on those two to do great things. I'll wrap it up with a few more of my student athletes that make my work special: Taylor West who finally is starting to roar and the Beard brothers Russell and William that work so well together as brothers, friends, and competitors. And then there is the Oakman 3, Zach, AJ, and Ashley. Over the past 25 years I have had to opportunity to influence, guide, lead, and mentor over 1000 plus student athletes playing 10 different sports at the high school, collegiate and professional levels. I would have loved to name them all, but that would be another book in itself. However, each student athlete is important to me and I am grateful to each of them for the lessons I have learned through working with them. They are my purpose they are my legacy.

I'm blessed to live my purpose every day. So, I will give all that I have and will continue to do so for as long as I can. The most important two days of anyone's life is the day they are born and the day they find out why. Live your purpose.

Scribbles and Doodles

How do you define mentorship and what role does it play in your life? Do you live your definition of mentorship daily?

____

____

____

____

____

____

____

____

____

____

As a mentor what are some of the tools you provide in order for your mentee to succeed?

____

____

____

____

____

____

____

____

____

____

As a mentee list 3 tools that your mentor has provided that has helped you to learn and grow in the past 6 months.

____
____
____
____
____
____
____
____
____
____

Final Thoughts:

____
____
____
____
____
____
____
____
____
____

CHAPTER 3

Principles for Mentoring

When it comes to mentoring there are several principles that I like to consider in order to ensure that the mentee is getting the very best that I have to offer. To lead, guide, and encourage consistently at any level requires making sure as a mentor, you provide information that the mentee can use immediately as well as long term to achieve their goals personally and professionally. The following principles are key cornerstones for the foundation for a successful mentor / mentee relationship.

1. **Respect:** A mentor should respect the mentee's goals, perspectives, and needs, and should be open to learning as well. Respect is a key principle of mentoring as it is essential for building a strong and productive relationship between the mentor and the mentee. Respect means treating the mentee with dignity and valuing their ideas, experiences, and opinions. It also involves acknowledging the mentee's strengths and capabilities, and recognizing their potential for growth and development. A mentor who shows respect for their mentee is more likely to gain their trust and build a positive and supportive relationship. In turn, the mentee should also show respect for the mentor's time, expertise, and role as a guide and mentor. By showing mutual respect, the mentee and mentor can work together effectively and achieve their goals.

2. **Trust:** A strong mentoring relationship is built on trust, and a mentor should be reliable, dependable, and trustworthy. Trust is a key principle of mentoring, as it is essential for the mentee to feel comfortable sharing their goals, challenges, and experiences with their mentor. A mentee who trusts their mentor is more likely to be open and honest with them, which is essential for the mentor to be able to provide effective guidance and support. Trust is built over time through consistent, honest, and supportive interactions between the mentor and the mentee. A mentor who is reliable, consistent, and respectful can help to build trust with their mentee. In turn, the mentee should also act in a trustworthy manner, by following through on commitments, being honest and open with the mentor, and maintaining confidentiality as appropriate. Trust is a foundation for a strong and productive mentoring relationship.

3. **Communication:** Effective communication is essential in a mentoring relationship, and a mentor should be able to listen actively and provide feedback and guidance in a constructive and supportive manner. Effective communication is a key principle of mentoring, as it is essential for building a strong and productive relationship between the mentor and the mentee. Communication involves listening actively and attentively to the mentee, asking questions to better understand their goals and challenges, and providing feedback in a constructive and supportive way. A mentor who communicates effectively can help their mentee to feel heard and understood, and can provide value insights and

guidance based on their own experiences and expertise. In turn, the mentee should also communicate openly and honestly with their mentor, sharing their goals, challenges, and experiences, and seeking feedback and guidance as needed. Good communication is essential for building a strong and productive mentoring relationship.

4. **Confidentiality:** A mentor should respect the confidentiality of the mentee, and should not disclose personal or sensitive information without the mentee's permission. Confidentiality is a key principle of mentoring, as it is essential for a mentee to feel safe and secure in sharing sensitive or personal information with their mentee. A mentor should respect the mentee's privacy and confidentiality, and should not disclose any information shared by the mentee without their explicit permission. Confidentiality is important for building trust and creating a safe space for the mentee to share their thoughts and experiences. In turn, the mentee should also respect the confidentiality of the mentoring relationship, and should not disclose any information shared by the mentor without their permission. By maintaining confidentiality, the mentee and mentor can create a safe and supportive environment in which the mentee can feel comfortable seeking guidance and support.

5. **Empathy:** A mentor should be able to understand and empathize with the mentee's experiences and challenges, and should be able to provide support and encouragement. Empathy is a key

principle of mentoring, as it involves the ability to understand and share the feelings and experiences of the mentee. A mentor who is empathetic can better understand the mentee's perspective, and can provide more targeted and effective guidance and support. Empathy also involves being able to listen actively and attentively to the mentee, and to show understanding and compassion for their challenges and struggles. By demonstrating empathy, a mentor can help the mentee to feel heard and understood, and create a sense of trust and rapport in the mentoring relationship. In turn, the mentee should also be empathetic towards their mentor, and should show understanding and appreciation for their time, efforts, and expertise.

6. **Goal-oriented:** A mentor should help the mentee to identify and pursue their goals, and should provide guidance and support as the mentee works towards those goals. Being goal-oriented is a key principle of mentoring as it involves helping the mentee to set and work towards specific goals that will help them to grow and develop both personally and professionally. A mentor should work with the mentee to identify their goals and aspirations, and should help them to develop a plan to achieve those goals. This may involve providing guidance and advice, offering resources or connections, and helping the mentee to overcome challenges or obstacles. By setting and working towards specific goals, the mentee can make progress and achieve success, and can feel a sense of accomplishment and satisfaction. In turn, the mentor should also be goal-oriented, and

should work with the mentee to set and track progress towards their goals.

7. **Flexibility:** A mentor should be flexible and adaptable, and should be able to adjust their approach to fit the needs and preferences of the mentee. Flexibility is a key principle of mentoring as it involves being open to adapting to the needs and preferences of the mentee. A mentor should be willing to adjust their approach based on the individual needs and goals of the mentee, and should be open to exploring different strategies and resources to support their development. This may involve being flexible with the frequency and format of meetings, or being open to trying new approaches or techniques to help the mentee achieve their goals. By being flexible, a mentor can better support the mentee's growth and development, and can help to create a productive and effective mentoring relationship. In turn, the mentee should also be flexible and open to trying new approaches and techniques, and should be willing to adapt their goals and plans as needed.

8. **Professionalism:** A mentor should be professional and adhere to ethical standards in the mentoring relationship. Professionalism is a key principle of mentoring, as it involves maintaining high standards of conduct and performance in the mentoring relationship. A mentor should act in a professional manner, which may include being punctual and reliable, maintaining confidentiality, and providing constructive and respectful feedback. A mentor should also strive to be a role model for their

mentee, demonstrating professionalism in their own work and behavior. By being professional, a mentor can set a positive example for the mentee and help them to develop their own professional skills and standards. In turn, the mentee should also act in a professional manner, by being respectful and attentive, following through on commitments, and maintaining confidentiality as appropriate.

These are a few of the many principles that are important in mentoring. An effective mentor should be able to demonstrate these principles and apply them in a way that is appropriate and helpful to the mentee. Also, remember to utilize the following principles:

- Be honest with correction and praise to the mentee.
- Give the mentee both recognition and praise.
- Have a perspective of where you and the mentee are trying to go.
- As a mentor develop people always and manage things.
- As a mentor your mentee is an opportunity, not an interruption.

Principles are important in mentoring because they provide a foundation for the mentoring relationship and guide the actions and behaviors of both the mentor and the mentee. Principles can help establish trust, respect, and understanding between the two parties and ensure that the mentoring relationships is productive and beneficial for both individuals. Principles can also help mentors and mentees set goals, communicate effectively, and provide support and guidance to one another.

Overall, principles are crucial for ensuring that a mentoring relationship is healthy, effective, and mutually beneficial.

A story of principles:

Pat Williams has been a cornerstone of support, information and mentor in my life. I often say he reinforced all of things taught to me by my parents, grandparents, coaches, and neighbors about betting on myself. Pat was clear and concise in mentoring me on the importance of being a professional. His advice was to treat every day as though it was the championship and that winning and success was directly related to my mental and physical preparation. Most people fail because of their lack of being willing to prepare for success. Pat helped me to develop and refine the tools I needed to stay inspired, encouraged and driven even through adversity. His thought process was amateurs practice to get it right, professionals practice to never get it wrong. This thought process helped me to risk being great. If you risk nothing, do nothing, you get nothing. Professionals focus and execute regardless of who is watching. Pat would say, "The truth of the matter Almon, there is always someone watching." So, knowing that someone is always watching is where I further developed my lead with your life mentality. One of Pat's favorite quotes is, "If it is to be it is up to me." by William H. Johnsen and that quote really resonates with me. I want to be the change that I want to see in the world. My story could be written best by me. I have full control of the narrative. I can always count on Pat to tell it to me straight, be there for me no matter what, and never stop cheering for me. He believed in my ability to be a servant leader, author, and dynamic speaker even before I did.

Great mentors know how to get the best out of you and
help you, get you to trust the process, do hard shit,
embrace hard talks, and never give up on what you say
you want. In the game of life, it's not where you start, it's
where you finish.

Scribbles and Doodles

How do you show respect as a mentor to your mentee? Or how do you show respect as a mentee to your mentor? (Give examples of both)

____

____

____

____

____

____

____

____

____

____

As a mentor or mentee, list 3 tools you use to be a better communicator?

____

____

____

____

____

____

____

____

____

____

Flexibility is directly related to your ability to be prepared. How do you prepare daily to succeed as a mentor or mentee?

____

____

____

____

____

____

____

____

____

Final Thoughts:

____

____

____

____

____

____

____

____

____

CHAPTER 4

Principles to Strengthen Mentoring

To be a successful mentor on a more consistent basis it is important that you work to strengthen your mentoring skills. If you are going to be responsible for helping someone to grow personally and professionally, you must be willing to work on the skills that will make you a stronger leader. The following are some principles needed to strengthen the mentoring skills of the mentor: Clear Communication, Active Listening, Goal-Setting, Providing Guidance, Providing Resources, Providing Feedback, Building Trust, and Continual Learning.

Clear Communication: Establishing clear communication channels and setting expectations for meetings and feedback can help ensure a successful mentoring relationship. Clear communication is essential for a successful mentoring relationship. One way to improve communication is to establish clear channels of communication, such as setting regular meetings or check-ins. This ensures that both the mentor and the mentee are on the same page and can discuss any issues or concerns in a timely manner. It is also important to set expectations for communication, such as response times and preferred methods of communication. This can help ensure that everyone is aware of what is expected in terms of communication and can help avoid any confusion or misunderstandings.

Active listening is another important aspect of clear communication. Encourage the mentee to share their thoughts ideas, and concerns, and actively listen to them. This will help build trust and mutual understanding. Additionally, it's important to avoid interrupting, and instead, ask clarifying questions and reflect back to the mentee what you heard. This shows that you are engaged and interested in what they have to say. By actively listening, the mentor can identify any potential problems or misunderstandings, and address them before they become bigger issues.

Another important aspect of clear communication is to be clear and concise when communicating. Avoid using jargon or technical language that may be confusing to the mentee, and instead, use simple and straightforward language. Additionally, it's important to be direct and honest in your communication, even when delivering difficult or negative feedback. This helps to avoid confusion and ensures that everyone is on the same page. Being clear and direct in your communication can also help establish a culture of open and honest communication, which is essential for a successful mentoring relationship.

Lastly, effective communication is a two-way street, so it is important for the mentor to be open to feedback and willing to adjust their communication style as needed. The mentee may have a different communication style and it's important for the mentor to be aware of that and adapt accordingly. Encourage the mentee to provide feedback on the communication style and make adjustments as necessary. This can ensure that the mentee feels comfortable and heard, which can help build trust and foster a more effective mentoring relationship.

Active Listening: Encourage the mentee to share their thoughts, ideas, and concerns and actively listen to them. This will help build trust and mutual understanding. It is important that you pay attention to the speaker. One of the most important aspects of being an active listener is paying attention to the person who is speaking. This means setting aside distractions, such as your phone or other electronic devices, and focusing solely on the speaker. It also means maintaining eye contact and using body language, such as nodding or making small facial expressions, to show that you are engaged in the conversation.

Avoid interrupting the mentee when they are speaking. Interrupting someone while they are speaking can be rude and can disrupt the flow of the conversation. Instead, allow the speaker to finish their thoughts before responding. This will also give you more time to process the information and come up with a thoughtful response.

Asking questions is the best way to gather additional information. It is a great way to show that you are actively listening and engaged in the conversation. It also helps to clarify any points that you may not fully understand. However, it is important to avoid asking too many questions as this can make the conversation feel more like an interrogation.

Reflect on what is being said: Reflecting on what the speaker is saying is an effective way to show that you are actively listening. This can be done by paraphrasing what the speaker has said or by summarizing the main points. Reflecting on what is being said can also help to build deeper understanding of the conversation.

As tempting as it may be, don't multitask. It is important to avoid multitasking while actively listening. This means not doing other tasks, such as checking your phone or responding to emails, while someone is speaking to you. This can be very disrespectful and can make it difficult to pay attention to the conversation. Instead, give the conversation your undivided attention to be a more active listener.

In summary, the key to being a more active listener is to pay attention to the speaker, avoid interrupting, ask questions, reflect on what is being said, and avoid multitasking. By practicing these habits, you can improve your listening skills and have more productive and meaningful conversations.

Goal-Setting: Setting specific, measurable, achievable, relevant, and time-bound (SMART) goals can help both the mentor and mentee stay focused and track progress. Start by setting specific, measurable, and achievable goals. Instead of saying "I want to be healthier," set a specific goal like "I will lose 10 pounds in the next three months." This makes it clear what you're working towards and allows you to track your progress.

Make sure your goals are aligned with your values and long-term vision. It's important to set goals that align with what you truly want in life, rather than what you think you should want or what others want for you. This will give you more motivation to achieve them.

Break down your goals into smaller, manageable steps. This will make your goals feel less overwhelming and give you a sense of accomplishment as you make progress. For example, if your goal is to write a book, break it down into smaller goals like writing a chapter a month or completing a set number of pages each week. As the old saying goes, "The best way to eat an elephant, is one bite at a time." Don't get ahead of yourself when pursuing your goals. Focus on getting 1% better each day.

Hold yourself accountable by setting deadlines and creating a plan of action. This will keep you motivated and on track towards achieving your goals. Be sure to review your progress regularly and make adjustments as needed.

Finally, remember that goal setting is a continuous process and it's important to adjust and adapt your goals as you progress. Be open to change and be willing to adjust your goals as needed. Remember that failure is not a setback but an opportunity to learn and grow. Stay flexible, stay determined, stay focused and you will be a great goal setter.

Providing Guidance: Give guidance and support to the mentee, but also allow them to make their own decisions and learn from their experiences. One of the most important principles of being a mentor is providing guidance to the mentee. This means that the mentor should be able to offer advice and support to help the mentee navigate their professional or personal development. This guidance can take many forms, including providing feedback on work or offering suggestions for improvement, providing resources or connections, and helping the mentee set and achieve goals.

Another important aspect of providing guidance as a mentor is being a good listener. A mentor should be able to actively listen to the mentee's concerns and ideas, and offer support and guidance based on what the mentee is telling them. This means that a mentor should be able to put aside their own biases and opinions, and truly listen to what the mentee has to say.

Providing guidance as a mentor also means being honest and direct with the mentee. A mentor should be able to provide constructive criticism and feedback, even if it may be difficult for the mentee to hear. This honesty and directness can help the mentee improve and grow in their personal and professional development.

Another key principle of providing guidance as a mentor is being available and responsive. A mentor should be able to make themselves available to the mentee when they need help or support, and respond to their questions or concerns in a timely manner. This availability and responsiveness, helps to build trust and a strong relationship between the mentor and mentee.

Finally, providing guidance as a mentor means being a role model for the mentee. A mentor should be able to demonstrate the values and behaviors that they are trying to teach the mentee. By being a good role model, the mentor can help to inspire the mentee to strive for similar success in their own personal and professional development.

Providing Resources: Provide the mentee with resources and information that will help them achieve their goals and develop their skills. One of the key principles of being a mentor is providing resources to the mentee. This means that the mentor should be able to offer the mentee access to information, tools, and connections that will help them navigate their professional or personal development. This can include providing access to books, articles, or online resources, connecting the mentee with other professionals or experts in their field, or providing access to networking events or professional development opportunities.

Providing resources as a mentor also means being able to offer advice and support on specific issues or challenges that the mentee may be facing. This can include helping the mentee with job search, career advice, or giving insights on a specific industry. A mentor should be able to provide the mentee with the knowledge and tools they need to make informed decisions and take action on their goals.

One of the key benefits of providing resources as a mentor is that it allows the mentee to take an active role in their own learning and development. Rather than simply telling the mentee what they need to know or do, the mentor is giving them the tools and resources to learn and grow on their own. This can be particularly effective for mentees who are self-motivated and eager to learn.

Another important aspect of providing resources as a mentor is being able to connect the mentee with other people in their field or industry. This can include connecting the mentee with other professionals, experts, or mentors who can offer additional support and guidance. This kind of networking can help the mentee to expand their professional network, and open up new opportunities for growth and advancement.

It is important to note that providing resources as a mentor is not a one-time event, it should be an ongoing process. The mentor should be constantly updating their mentee with new resources that are relevant to their mentee's development. This allows the mentee to stay current with the latest trends, knowledge and skills in their field. With the fast-paced changes in technology, it is important for mentors to be able to help mentee to stay up-to-date with the latest tools, applications and resources that can help them to be more effective in their work and personal life.

Finally, being able to provide resources as a mentor means being able to offer support and guidance on a wide range of topics. A mentor should be able to provide the mentee with resources and advice on a variety of issues, including career development, personal growth, and work-life balance. This means being able to offer a diverse range of resources that can meet the mentee's needs as they evolve over time.

Providing Feedback: Give feedback on the mentee's progress and performance in a constructive and supportive manner. The principle of providing feedback as a mentor is a vital aspect of mentorship. It involves giving constructive and actionable feedback to mentees to help them improve their skills and achieve their goals.

First and foremost, feedback should always be given in a timely manner. This means that mentors should not wait until the end of a project or mentorship to give feedback, but rather provide it throughout the process. This allows mentees to make necessary adjustments and improvements in real-time.

Additionally, feedback should be specific and clear. This means that mentors should avoid vague or general statements and instead focus on specific areas of improvement. For example, instead of saying "you need to work on your communication skills," a mentor could say "I noticed that you had trouble articulating your ideas during the team meeting. It would be helpful if you could practice summarizing your thoughts in a clear and concise manner before the next meeting."

It is also important for mentors to provide a balance of positive and negative feedback. While it is important to address areas of improvement, it is also crucial to recognize and celebrate the mentee's accomplishments and strengths. This helps to build their confidence and motivation.

Finally, providing feedback as a mentor requires active listening and engagement. A mentor should be attentive and responsive to their mentee's needs and provide feedback in a way that is respectful and supportive. This creates a safe and open environment for mentees to receive feedback, and allows them to feel comfortable asking for help and guidance.

Building Trust: Building trust is essential for a successful mentoring relationship. It can be built by being consistent, reliable and transparent. Building trust as a mentor is essential for a successful mentoring relationship. Trust is the foundation upon which a mentee can feel safe and comfortable sharing their thoughts, ideas, and concerns with their mentor. Without trust, a mentee may not feel comfortable sharing their vulnerabilities or asking for help, which can limit the potential of the mentoring relationship.

One way to build trust as a mentor is through consistency and reliability. This means being dependable, keeping your commitments, and following through on your promises. By showing that you can be counted on, a mentee will be more likely to trust you and feel comfortable opening up to you.

Another way to build trust as a mentor is through active listening. This means truly listening to your mentee and showing that you understand their perspective. By actively listening, you demonstrate that you value their ideas and opinions, which can help to build trust.

Being open and transparent is also important for building trust as a mentor. This means being honest and upfront about your own experiences, both positive and negative. By being open and transparent, you demonstrate that you are comfortable sharing your own vulnerabilities and that you are approachable.

Finally, building trust as a mentor also means being supportive and non-judgmental. This means being there for your mentee, providing guidance and encouragement, and being understanding when things don't go as planned. By being supportive and non-judgmental, you create a safe space for your mentee to share their thoughts and ideas, which can help to build trust.

Continual Learning: Continual learning is important for the mentor as well as mentee. This can help the mentor to stay updated with the latest knowledge and skills in the field. The principle of continual learning refers to the ability of a system or individual to continuously improve their knowledge and skills over time, without the need for explicit instruction or supervision. This is an important concept in the field of artificial intelligence and machine learning, as it allows machines to adapt to new tasks and environments without the need for extensive retraining.

One key aspect of continual learning is the ability to learn from experience. This means that a system or individual is able to take in new information and adjust their behavior or decision-making based on past experiences. This is especially important for tasks that are dynamic and changing, such as image recognition or natural language processing.

Another important aspect of continual learning is the ability to transfer knowledge. This means that a system or individual is able to use knowledge acquired in one task or environment to improve performance in another. For example, a machine learning model trained on images of cats may be able to use that knowledge to improve its performance on images of dogs.

A third aspect of continual learning is the ability to handle catastrophic forgetting. This refers to the phenomenon where a system or individual forgets previously learned information when learning new information. It is a major challenge in continual learning and can be addressed using techniques such as regularization or the use of a memory bank.

In conclusion, the principle of continual learning is an important concept that allows systems and individuals to continuously adapt and improve their knowledge and skills over time. As a mentor, it is important to be aware of these concepts and to help guide and support individuals in developing their own capacity for continual learning.

Story number one:

A story on strengthening the principle of mentorship.

About 10 years ago I was training one of my athletes and there was a conditioning camp going on with about 150 student athletes of all ages on the same field in which I was training. When I finished my session and started walking off the field, I heard someone yell, "Hey Coach." As I turned and looked it was a pretty big guy running towards me who was running the camp yelling, 'Wait up." He caught up to me an introduced himself. He said, "I am Coach Rodney Blunt." And as I went to introduce myself, he said, "Coach everyone knows who you are." That statement was funny to me because I always flew under the radar. I never advertised that I worked with student athletes but yet Coach Blunt knew. He said he wanted to run some things by me and asked if we could do lunch and I said of course. We picked a day, time and place and connected. Coach told me he started a non-profit called City Streets 2 Student Athletes and the mission of the organization was to help student athletes live a drug free life. I was totally on board with that. Coach Blunt is a DEA agent so if anyone knows how drugs can destroy lives, Coach certainly does. He is on the front line every day fighting to keep kids safe. I encourage everyone who is reading this story to go to www.cs2sa.com and check out what Coach Blunt is doing. Also support his organization because everyone of us knows someone who has been affected by drugs.

In our meeting coach asked me questions about how to build an organization, develop leadership, get people on board with what he's doing, etcetera. The first thing I said to coach was, "I will tell you everything I know about working with kids, parents, schools, and organizations. I'll give you the information and then you get to make the decisions you want with it." I told coach that life is about information and decision making. Secondly, I told coach, "Do what you say you will do." Your word is everything. Coach Blunt said, "Coach you are never going to be able to shake me. I am in your pocket." And a mentor / mentee relationship was born. Coach Blunt and I have incredible trust in each other. He is always open to feedback and has a willingness to learn like nothing I have ever seen. We came together and utilized every resource that was available to help move the mission of City Street forward. Coach is a life-long learner. Every day he puts himself in the position to learn, risk and grow so he can pass it on to others. Throughout the year City Streets does camps and a summer bus tour to help student athletes to grow as tall as they possibly can.

Today Coach Blunt is one day closer to the next chapter of his life as a coach, speaker, and author. I encourage him every day to write his own story, because that is truly the only way to have a legacy that never ends. Principles such as seeking guidance, welcoming feedback, and being a life-long learner is how the good becomes great. As a mentor / mentee surround yourself with positive people who are driven, committed, and servant leaders of people. As I always say to Coach Blunt, "Be the change you want to see in the world. Always lead with your life."

Story number two:

In February of 2022 I had the opportunity to speak for the non-profit Ounce of Prevention Fund of Florida. While there I met a young man named Kevian Prather (KP). Turns out KP was a teacher and coach in Valdosta Georgia and we had the opportunity to talk about student athletes, coaching, and leadership. Right off the bat I liked Coach KP's enthusiasm for working with student athletes and his desire to learn and grow to be better. He asked if I would be his mentor and of course I said I will share with you what I know. We connected and one weekend he came down to Jacksonville because he wanted to see one of my training sessions, because like most people he couldn't quite see how training using only cones and yardsticks could get the job done. Well, KP decided to do the training instead of just watching it and let's just say he found out pretty quickly that a lot of training can happen in 30 seconds. He has been an absolute sponge, absorbing everything I throw at him. He took the training techniques that I showed him and incorporated them into what he was already doing and needless to say it's a hit.

KP has an incredible company in Valdosta named Technique Athletes Inc. He is building strong young men and women. I encourage you to go to his website and check out the things he is doing in and out of his community www.techniqueathletesinc.com. We now do an annual camp titled Iron Sharpens Iron Development Camp that focuses on building a solid foundation centered around character, speed, agility, quickness, and mental toughness. Coach KP is definitely getting 1% better each day and is living the principles of strengthening mentorship.

Scribbles and Doodles

As a mentor or mentee what tools do you use to continually build trust and respect?

____

____

____

____

____

____

____

____

____

____

As a mentor or mentee, list 3 principles for strengthening mentorship that you feel are vital in order to be successful?

____

____

____

____

____

____

____

____

____

As a mentor or mentee how do provide and or receive feedback?

____

____

____

____

____

____

____

____

____

Final Thoughts:

____

____

____

____

____

____

____

____

____

CHAPTER 5

Leadership Matters In Mentoring

Being a mentor requires having certain characteristics that lend themselves to helping an individual develop and grow as tall and wide as he or she possibly can. As a mentor having the right characteristics to help a mentee to succeed is like anything else in life that you desire to be good at, you have to work at it. Great characteristics don't just happen. You have to develop them. As a mentor the best way to ensure that you are leading in the right way, is to always be the change you want to see in the world or simply put lead with your life!

As a leader it is important to understand that, "Leadership is supposed to be the passage of power from one person to another. Not conquering people through victory." Leadership that focuses on mentoring will always produce more leaders. When we try to run the race alone, we will most likely end up going fast but ending up nowhere. Often times we fail to lead others because we lack good mentors and therefore, we produce no leaders. And where there are no leaders there will be no legacy.

In Chapter 2 I discussed leadership and the importance it plays in having a lasting legacy, but let's dig a little deeper. Leadership first and foremost is an action not a position. Successful leaders take action by doing what they say they will do. They are willing to lead the way by doing not just talking. Mentees need leadership that is action driven in order to continue to learn, risk, and grow.

Leadership in the world today seems to lack that action and passion that I grew up witnessing. The notion of it takes a village to raise and develop productive young men and women is long gone. I grew up in a time when I was constantly reminded by my papa that someone has to be first if we are to progress in any form, shape or fashion. What my papa meant was at some point you have to be willing to take action, you have to be willing to bet on yourself and put it all on the line. Talk is cheap. Making bold statements may sound good, but they are nothing more than hot air if you don't take bold action. Complaining about a situation doesn't change the situation. The only way to bring about change is to always lead with your life and be the change you want to see in the world.

Leaders like Frederick, Douglass, Carter G Woodson, Harriet Tubman, Malcolm X, Dr, Martin Luther King Jr, and Ida B Wells just to name a few were not afraid to be first. They understood the assignment and embraced all that came with being out front. Each knew his or her value and each never went seeking to be leaders. Successful leaders emerge from doing the work. In a sea of green they paint themselves purple by connecting their words and actions. When vision, communication of that vision, competence, passion, the right people skills, being bold, and being a servant of and for the people intersect, you end up with a servant leader. You end up with a mentor to many. A person whos' legacy will be pasted down from generation to generation.

We have failed to produce these types of leaders consistently because the art of mentorship got lost. We somehow neglected to give back, to share the information in a way that inspired others to continue to knock down barriers, and sacrifice whatever was needed to move the world forward. People who wanted to be better and do better, forgot to ask to be mentored by some of the greatest leaders of all time so we are still stuck in first gear.

To develop strong leadership that serves in every capacity, there are several things we need to do better:

1. We need to make sure we are providing the tools and resources that are needed to produce good leaders. Without good leaders to model the way the next generation will make the same mistakes as the previous leaders and will lack authenticity to make new mistakes. Which also means we will lack good people to mentor others. (Sometimes as a leader it is more important for you to do versus say. Let your work speak for you.)

2. We need to develop leaders that have great habits that inspire others to want to replicate them. Virtues such as being: trustworthy, respectful, disciplined, focused, timely, committed, determined, and persistent. These are all virtues that have stood the test of time.

3. We must be willing to share our knowledge and authority. Successful leaders are willing to delegate and empower others to move things forward. As a leader the only way you can pick something else up is to free your hands. So always be willing to let go of things that will not only help others grow, but will allow you to grow as well. Don't be afraid to share power.

4. We need to develop and distribute a formal training program that will guide and help others to achieve their goals. A clear concise training

program will allow for greater consistency in creating successful leaders.

5. We must know our value so we have the willingness to let go of things that sabotage progress. When what you do is how you see your value to an organization, you will never let go. Your value as a person should never be linked to what you do or do not do for a living.

6. Be confident in who you are. Only confident people affirm others. When you are confident you have the ability to say great job to others and mean it. As a leader there should never be an absence of confirmation.

7. Focus on developing people skills because in the end developing people is what really matters. Successful leaders do not put paper work before people work. People are and always will be the driving force that is needed to make things better.

8. We should always encourage debate. Dictatorship in decision making will never produce more leaders. The goal is always to become an organization of leaders, not an organization with a leader. Buy-in from others can go a long way in achieving organizational and personal goals.

9. We need to be open to the possibilities of what the universe brings. Every now and then a maverick shows up and we would be wise to listen. It may

turn out to be the very ride the organization needs to take to grow.

My papa used to say, "If you going to build something right, you need the right tools." In order for a mentee to grow into the leader he or she is destined to be, they must have the right tools. As a leader providing the right tools is only the first step, the second and most important step is teaching the mentee how to use the tools to his or her benefit to become a servant leader. Mastering how to utilize the tools of leadership requires repetition, repetition, repetition. The mentee has to be willing to sacrifice all that he or she has in order to learn and the mentor has to be willing to sacrifice all that he or she has to teach. The next generation of leaders will be only as good as the tools they have to build the bridges that are needed for others to cross.

Great habits are developed through being disciplined. Success is a by-product of consistently doing the things that help you to be 1% better each day. Doing the work daily is a combination of courage, discipline, sacrifice, and respect. As leaders modeling these four things requires being trustworthy, committed, and persistent in what you do and in what you say. Mentees need to see good habits being demonstrated every day, not just being talked about. As the old saying goes, I would rather see a good sermon being demonstrated, than hearing a good sermon being talked about. Mentees need to be able to replicate good habits that will elevate them to be the leaders they want to be. Leaders should always say, be, and do, as if the whole world is watching.

As a leader, empowering others is one of the greatest gifts you can give. When you empower others what you are saying is I believe in you. You allow the individual to learn, risk, and grow in a way that when done right helps their confidence and self-esteem. Letting go isn't easy, but when you have provided the right tools and model the habits necessary to succeed you have to be willing to get out of the way and let the mentee shine. As a leader at some point your leadership skills will be tested. Every leader at some point in time will have the opportunity to either create more leaders and continue a legacy of servant leadership that lives beyond him or her or have the knowledge to die when he or she does. Building people will always be better than building buildings.

Successful leaders have a process they trust. Whether it be through trial and error, a mentor, or other opportunities, they discover a process that allows them to get 1% better each day. Most successful people journal or write things down which usually leads to discovering a pattern of behavior that leads to success. As a mentor using this information to create a roadmap for others can be priceless. When we formalize what we do and put it into a structured program for others to follow, it creates a system that allows others to learn, risk, and grow at a greater rate. More importantly it creates consistency in the tools that are being used and developed as well as, how good habits are being used to develop leaders.

The willingness to bet on yourself comes from knowing your value. When you know your value, you will always have a voice. When you look in the mirror you must realize that the person looking back at you matters. Leaders build people up by helping them to see that who they are and more importantly who they are not is what makes him or her special. Leaders inspire and encourage others to risk it all, but ultimately it is up to the mentee to believe in himself or herself. You're only as good as you believe you are. A major catalyst for me starting my company 25 years ago was my papa saying, "Son if you want to know what you're worth, go out on your own. The best way to get what you want is to create it yourself." I took those words and I bet on myself. When you know your value, nothing can stop you. You can't put a price on being comfortable in your own skin. As my mother would say, "When you know, you know."

Confidence is directly related to preparation. When you are prepared you are more flexible which allows for greater confidence. Most people want to be successful however, they lack the will to prepare to be successful. Success takes what it takes. There are no shortcuts or easy buttons that will lead you to the road of success. When you are confident you realize that when success occurs it do so as a by-product of the journey. As mentors when we prepare mentees the right way, we also increase his or her confidence. Confident people more times than not help others and affirm others because they know who they are. They are not afraid to share they light, because in doing so they only make the world brighter. If you were a candle, you could light a million other candles and it wouldn't diminish your light, it would only make your light shine brighter. Prepare to compete each day and you will be confident. "Chance favors the prepared mind."

As a mentor it is important that you uplift, encourage, and support your mentee. These 3 things are so important because they remind us that no one wins alone. My mother would say, "You can do bad by yourself baby, but you can't win by yourself. No one wins by themselves." As a leader constantly evolving and working on your people skills is how you keep your mentee inspired, encouraged, and engaged. As a mentor and as a mentee I realize when I slow down to go fast, I learn, risk, and grow at a much faster rate. People skills develop over time through respect, patience, and tolerance.

If your desire is to become an organization with leaders verses an organization with a leader, encourage debate. Allow other voices to be heard. As a mentor being an active listener and allowing your mentee to be heard is a great way to build trust and respect. The goal is to always get buy-in from others if you want to achieve professional as well as personal goals. The answers you seek more times than not are always in the room. Leadership is something that everyone has an opportunity to grow into.

Successful leaders are always open to the possibilities. Every day we wake up we have a choice and a chance. We get to choose our attitude, behavior, and effort and we get to take a chance on chasing our dreams or not. Opportunities are all around us, the question is what are you doing with them. Are you busy complaining and comparing your life with others or are you grateful and appreciative for what the day brings. No matter what you choose, the truth of the matter is life goes on. It doesn't stop no matter how bad or good your day is.

Leadership matters in all we do. Without leadership nothing is possible. Someone has to be first, someone has to risk, someone has to display courage. So why not you?

A story on why leadership matters in mentoring.

2001 the year I met Dr. David Langston and Dr. Dennis Webber is the same year I met Casandra Jenkins (CJ). It was Dr. Langston who introduced me to CJ. She happened to also be a guest speaker at North Florida Community College the same day that I was in 2001 with Dr. Langston. CJ graduated from Florida State University and without a doubt the biggest Nole fan I ever met. We hit it off immediately and after presenting at NFCC we started to talk and CJ said, "You know AG you should really focus on doing more to help women sports." That statement took me by surprise because at the time I wasn't even sure I wanted to work with student athletes at all. CJ pointed out why she thought I should help develop female student athletes and then helped me to develop the tools I needed to be successful at it. She created opportunities and opened up doors that would allow me to be in the right place to be of service to others. Before I knew it, I was sponsoring student athletes to attend FSU women basketball camps, volleyball camps, softball camps, and track and field. I was speaking to female athletic teams about the importance of teamwork and leadership and with each passing day more and more female athletes were training with me. I woke up one day and literally 75 percent of all the student athletes I train were and are female.

CJ mentored me on networking throughout the university system (no one networks like CJ), and helped me to sharpen my tools on creating processes that were specific to the needs of female student athletes. CJ has been at the forefront of debating issues that matter for all student athletes. People trust her, because she leads with her life every day. I am truly blessed to know and learn from CJ, because quite frankly she is what a servant leader should be. I am not sure how she does it all, but she does and with a smile. As her mentee I have learned how compassion and empathy are the cornerstones of

Scribbles and Doodles

As a mentor or mentee what habits do you feel are the most beneficial for being a successful mentor or mentee?

____

____

____

____

____

____

____

____

____

____

As a mentor or mentee, list 3 things you feel will help you be more confident as a mentor or mentee?

____

____

____

____

____

____

____

____

____

____

As a mentor or mentee how do you develop or improve your people skills?

____
____
____
____
____
____
____
____
____
____

Final Thoughts:

____
____
____
____
____
____
____
____
____
____

CHAPTER 6

Characteristics of a Mentee

A mentee is someone who is seeking guidance and support from a mentor to help them to achieve their personal and professional goals. Mentoring relationships can be very rewarding for both parties, but it is important for the mentee to possess certain characteristics to ensure the relationship is successful. The following are 8 characteristics of a good mentee.

1. Openness: A mentee should be open to new ideas and willing to learn from their mentor's experiences. There are possibilities all around however, if you approach the mentor / mentee relationship with a closed mind, nothing substantial will grow. Starting at what I call Ground Zero is of the upmost importance if true growth is going to take place. Also, the mentee should be willing to listen to feedback and take constructive criticism. Feedback and constructive correction are vital to the growth process of any relationship. *"Never let the same dog bite you twice." Wilson Gunter*

2. Initiative: A mentee must be proactive in seeking out a mentor and taking the initiative to drive the relationship forward. They should be willing to set goals and take action towards achieving them. Being mentored doesn't just happen. As a mentee you have to be willing to take a risk to ask for what you want. Achieving goals personally and

professionally requires courage, discipline, and persistence. So, getting to where you want to be, requires help from others. As a mentee it is important to remember to have a good relationship requires doing the work each day that is necessary for continued growth towards your personal and professional goals. *"The answer is always no if you don't ask." Eunice M Gunter*

3. Curiosity: A mentee should be curious about their chosen field or industry and eager to learn more. They should be curious about the world around them and willing to ask questions to gain deeper understanding. The key to wanting to learn more is finding your work versus finding a job. Your work is what you were born to do. It's something that you are passionate about. You will always be driven when you find your work. You will seek knowledge, come early, stay late, and ask questions when it's something you want to do. You can never be fired from your work. You can only be fired from your job. Your work is who you are on the inside. That's what you want a mentor to help you to develop. *"Knowledge makes a man unfit to be a slave." Frederick Douglass*

4. Flexibility: A mentor should be flexible and adaptable to change. They should be willing to try new things and embrace new challenges, even if they are outside their comfort zone. To gain greater flexibility you have to be prepared. If you want to succeed you have to do hard shit sometimes. The willingness to prepare is the greatest singular thing you can do, if you want to be more flexible in the game of life. Success more

times than not, comes down to the WILL versus the skill. Live your life uncomfortably and your growth will be exponentially. *"Everyone wants to be a lion until they have to do lion shit." Almon W Gunter Sr.*

5. Accountability: A mentee should take responsibility for their actions and be accountable for their own success. They should be willing to set realistic goals and work towards them, taking ownership of their progress. No matter how you slice it, in the end you determine where you end up in the game of life. The good, bad, or ugly that happens in your life at some point becomes yours to celebrate, change, or accept. No one can make you feel a certain way or do certain things without your permission. Ultimately, we teach people how to treat us, so be willing to own the things you should. *"We all have shit. Be willing to shovel your own shit." Wilson Gunter*

6. Respect: A mentee should show respect for their mentor's time and expertise. They should be willing to listen to their mentor's advice and take it seriously, even if they don't always agree. Time is the one thing you cannot get back once you use it. It is my experience that you always give time to what you truly love. If someone is willing to invest their time in you, as a mentee be willing to listen well and pay close attention to the information you are receiving. Most people are not successful simply because they do not listen well. It's okay to disagree, but you should always remain respectful and grateful for the opportunity to engage in uncomfortable talks. *"Get here, be here, and*

leave here. (Get here on time, be present, focused, and engaged, and go home to people you love.) Wilson Gunter

7. Humility: A mentee should be humble and willing to learn from others. They should be open to feedback and willing to acknowledge their own opportunities for improvements and other areas for growth in their lives. The ability to process and accept feedback from others is how we grow the most. Though feedback can often make us uncomfortable, it is what gives us the answers and drive we need to overcome adversity and build something substantial. Special things are built when we learn to live uncomfortably. *"Nothing substantial will never be built on ease."* *Almon W Gunter Jr.*

8. Gratitude: A mentor should show gratitude for their mentor's time and expertise. They should be appreciative of the guidance and support they receive and be willing to give back in any way they can. An attitude of gratitude will take you places that your talent cannot. Showing appreciation for the bridges that are built for you to cross and then keeping that legacy alive by building bridges for others is how progress is continuously made. Be in the habit of serving others and you will build a legacy that outlives you for generations. *"Some of the bridges you build are not for you to cross. They are for other people. So, build the bridge anyway. "Eunice M Gunter*

As a mentee there are other principles that can make the mentor / mentee relationship stronger. The following are 12 additional principles to consider if you are the mentee.

1. As a mentee be willing to be open and embrace the mentor and what they have to say.
2. As a mentee know and accept that the mentor is acting in your best interest always.
3. As a mentee the ability and the will to accept the mentor's council is critical to the mentor / mentee relationship.
4. As a mentee never abuse the privileges extended to you by the mentor in the form of information or opportunities.
5. As a mentee you must be willing to pursue a mentor. Mentors don't just show up. You have to put yourself out there and invite them in.
6. As a mentee you must ask questions. Questions are the best tools for pursuing your dreams. Asking questions allows the mentor to share what they know.
7. As a mentee make a personal investment in pursuing a mentor. Be willing to find the answers. Nothing is yours until you understand it.
8. As a mentee your job is to learn from the mentor, not compete with them.
9. As a mentee never take advise or constructive criticism from the mentor personally. Feedback from the mentor is necessary for growth.
10. As a mentee you can never learn from someone you are jealous of, so never compare or be jealous of the success of your mentor.
11. As a mentee be willing to commit to the process of learning from your mentor, even if it requires

personal sacrifice. Success will always require sacrifice.

12. As a mentee honesty is the best policy with your mentor. A true mentor can handle your secrets. A mentor is there to improve you not to share your secrets with others.

Overall, being a good mentee requires a willingness to learn, an open mind, and a proactive attitude towards personal and professional development. By possessing these characteristics, a mentee can make the most of their mentoring relationship and achieve their goals with the help of their mentor.

A story on being a good mentee:

My youngest son Austin graduated from the University of Florida in 2021 and like all young graduates the questions becomes what's next? Aussie is a planner, he likes setting goals, but more importantly he embraces the work that is required to reach them. As always Aus hit the road running. In his first job out of college as he would say, "dad I'm making moves." He's been promoted a couple of times within a year but came to me and said he needed a mentor. Which he's had mentors his entire life, because his mother and I have always encouraged it, so I suggested a friend, colleague and a brother from another mother Paul Vann. Paul and I have been friends since 2001. He's a retired Lt Colonel in the US Airforce and a finance guy. Aus had expressed interest in going into the Airforce as an officer, so what better guy to mentor him than Paul. (A little side note: I am sure the curiosity of going into the Airforce came about because his older brother Tre' is in the Army, but that's fine by me. Whatever it takes to keep my boys thinking, growing together, pushing each other and encouraging each other.)

I gave Aus the contact information for Paul, he called, and an hour later Mr. Vann had become uncle Paul. And just like that a mentor / mentee relationship was formed. The two came up with a plan for how the relationship would work and they have been working that plan every since. Aus understands the commitment that is involved to be a good mentee. He respects uncle Paul's time and is grateful for the opportunity to have someone like Paul providing information that is shaping his life for the future he wants. I love the fact that he is now accountable to Paul and that he has to be an advocate for his life. Aus has always been curious, and open to learning new things. He is great listener and executes what he learns. The best thing about his relationship with Paul is that I am not involved. It's not me pushing him or taking the initiative doing things for him that he should be doing for himself. It's amazing the growth that occurs when you empower people to go be great.

Being a good mentee is not easy. It requires that you have to be open to ideas that may make you uncomfortable, it requires you to embrace feedback that might not always be what you want to hear, and more importantly to be a good mentee you have to hold yourself accountable for getting the work that's required to succeed done.

As a parent you want your kids to have the best chance to be great. For me realizing that I couldn't and can't do it all alone when it comes to raising my children, (and as a parent you never stop raising them) the best thing I could do was find the right people in the right village to help me raise them. So, as my children will tell you, they have a lot of aunts and uncles. I am grateful, blessed, and encouraged to know there are people like Paul who are willing to mentor, serve, and lead the next generation.

Scribbles and Doodles

As a mentee how do you maintain flexibility and accountability with your mentor?

____

____

____

____

____

____

____

____

____

____

As a mentor or mentee, what role has gratitude played in the mentor/mentee relationship(s) in your life?

____

____

____

____

____

____

____

____

____

As a mentor or mentee what 3 of the 12 principles of a mentee resonates the most with you? And why?

____

____

____

____

____

____

____

____

____

Final Thoughts:

____

____

____

____

____

____

____

____

____

CHAPTER 7

A Lasting Legacy

Creating a lasting legacy is something that many people strive for in their lives. However, building a legacy that truly endures requires a great deal of thought, effort, and dedication. Building a lasting legacy requires a deliberate effort to create a positive impact that endures long after an individual's lifetime. To build a lasting legacy, the first step is to identify a cause or a set of values that aligns with one's passions and beliefs. It is essential to be clear about the impact one wants to make, be it through charitable work, community development, or innovation. Once the goal is defined, it is crucial to develop a strategic plan to achieve it. This plan should outline the specific actions and resources required to achieve the desired impact. It should also include a timeline for execution and evaluation to ensure progress is being made.

To build a lasting legacy, one must be committed to ongoing growth and improvement. Continuous learning and personal development are crucial to staying relevant and effective in achieving the desired impact. Collaboration with others who share similar goals and vales can also enhance the impact and increase the chances of lasting success. You must stay focused on your goals, even in the face of challenges or setbacks. This requires a strong sense of determination and perseverance, as well as the ability to adapt and pivot when necessary. Finally, documenting and sharing one's journey can inspire future generations to continue the work and build upon the legacy, ensuring longevity.

To secure a lasting legacy requires drilling down deep to ensure that your foundation for your legacy is built on the bedrock. The following are several elements that are cornerstones to ensuring your legacy has a chance to last well beyond you.

1. Define your values: Begin by identifying the values that are most important to you. These may include things like integrity, honesty, kindness, creativity, perseverance, effort and so on. These values will serve as a guide for your actions and decisions. The values you define for yourself will set the tone for everything you do when creating your legacy. For me, respect, responsibility, attitude, behavior, and effort are key pieces of my value. Respect and responsibility are the two words that my mother stressed the most. She modeled what respect and responsibility looked like every day. I learned to respect me first, because without self-respect it was impossible to respect others. As my mother would say, "you can't give what you don't have." And secondly, be an advocate for your life. Learn to fight for what you want for yourself. In other words, you are responsible for the things you say, want, and do. In the end your life is a result of the information you received and the decisions that you made. Attitude as my papa would say comes in two flavors: Good or Bad. There are no in between. You either have a good attitude or a bad attitude and the good news is you decide which it is every day. You and you alone are responsible for what

kind of attitude you have. Behavior is decision making. My goal each day is to make the best decisions I can with the information I have. Sometimes I fall short, but the key is to own it. Don't point fingers at others or play the blame game. Learn and grow from it and move on. 1% better each day is my motto. Effort like attitude is you and you alone own every day. You get to decide what level of effort you will exhibit each day. For me your effort was 100% or not. It's easy thing to measure, because you either were 100% or not. The goal is 100%, so anything short of that doesn't count. When I display these. 5 things to the best of my ability each day, I know beyond a shadow of a doubt that I got 1% better. Then the next day I do it all over again. It is doing the little things each day that will have the greatest impact on your ability to succeed.

2. Set clear goals: Once you have identified your values, set clear and achievable goals that align with those values. These goals should be specific, measurable, and have a timeline for completion. When it comes to goal setting, I find that most people start out with the best of attentions, but somehow let setbacks, bumps in the road, or adversity deter them from moving forward. First and foremost, always talk yourself in to your goals not out of them. When adversity strikes (and it will) it is so easy to think about all of the reasons you should quit or give up. But when this moment happens you have to remember why you chose the goal, what it means to achieve it, and how it benefits and impact not only your life but other's lives. Talk yourself into staying your course. My

mother use to say, "the best way out of something is to go through it." With adversity comes opportunity for growth. Your strength will never come from winning. Your strength will always come from the adversity that you faced and how hard you fought to get through the other side of it. Build in checkpoints for completing milestones, but don't panic if you are not where you thought you would be. Success takes time. Sometimes you have to slow down in order to go fast. Focus on controlling the things that you can control. You are not competing against the world you are competing against yourself. The great thing about setting goals are they are yours. You get to choose, you get to decide what's important to you, and you ultimately are the one that has to do the work. Not everyone will see your vision, not everyone will cheer for you to succeed, but pursue your vision, trust your training, and succeed anyway. "It's not where you start, it's where you finish."

3. Take action: Act on your goals and values consistently over time. Make choices that reflect your values, and take steps toward achieving your goals every day. Remember that small actions over time can lead to significant results. My papa used to say, "son you know what happens when you do a little thing consistently right over time? It's no longer a little thing." I have learned to do the little things that most people forget about doing. The fundamentals of anything are the foundation of that thing and when executed to perfection success is the result. Successful people know how to go beyond boredom. They

can do the monotonous thing that would drive the average person insane, day after day after day, but that's the key to their success. The lack of discipline destroys most dreams. Having a goal is just the beginning. You can dream it, see it, believe it, tell it, and plan it, but at some point, you have to do it. Nothing is a success until it is done. No matter how much you plan until you take action towards that plan you will not know does it really work. To take action is to take a risk, but risk must be taken if goals are to be met. Your progress in achieving anything can only be measured when you take action. Getting 1% percent better each day or eating an elephant one bite at a time doesn't sound like much, until you do it each and every day over time. You will always get out of life what you put in. If you risk nothing, do nothing, you get nothing. Every day means every day. Legacies are not built over night. They are built over time. Do the work.

4. Share your knowledge and expertise: Share what you know and have learned with others. This could be through teaching, mentoring, or volunteering in your community. Everything I am today is a result of the information I received from my mother, father, grandparents, aunts, uncles, coaches, mentors, and neighbors. Information is the most important thing you can receive, because with information, understanding, and action you make your story whatever you want it to be. Our legacy is built on what we shared and done for others. My great-great-great grandfather's legacy is still thriving today because it lives within me. Because of the information that

was passed down from generation to generation, his values and principles are still being taught. I have learned through my many mentors that life is about building bridges. Bridges are how we connect, enrich, and inspire others to continue to learn, risk, and grow. Progress is made when knowledge is shard and wisdom is gained. Through mutual respect, intentional conversation, intentional understanding, and intentional action progress is made. When you fail to continue to learn you allow fear to consume your life. More times than not we are most afraid of the unknown. So, this fact alone is the reason we should always seek knowledge. Education makes it impossible for a person to be a slave. My mother reminded me when needed that A) contrary to my belief, it's not about me, it's about helping other people B) some of the bridges you build are not for you to cross, they are for other people. So, build them anyway. I am blessed because so many people took the time to build bridges for me to cross. So, every day I lead with my life building bridges and providing whatever meaningful information I can to inspire and help others to write their own story. Afterall, the information doesn't belong to me, it belongs to God. The assignment was passed down to me from generation after generation after generation to serve others. And I understand the assignment very well. Therefore, I will get 1 % better every day, lead with my life always, share what I know each day, and build bridges whenever and where ever I can.

5. Build meaningful relationships: Build strong and meaningful relationships with those around you.

This includes family, friends, colleagues, and your community. Treat others with respect, kindness, and empathy. Life is about the relationships you have. You become what you consistently hang around. If you spend your time with 9 lazy people, you will eventually become number 10. Show me your friends and I will show you your future. My mentor Pat Williams in one of our very first sessions told me, "with the right relationship with just 2 people you can build a great business." Let me tell you, he was spot on. When you find people that believe in you, who are not afraid to have the hard talks with you, and only agenda is to help you grow, you have something truly special. However, great relationships don't just happen. Whether you are talking personal or professional relationship you have to work at it. Each day you have to be what you want to see. As my mother would say, "it doesn't cost anything to be kind." It boils down to how you see and feel about yourself. You have to love you before you can truly love others. The longer I live the more I realize that the best relationships are built on doing the little things. And to practice doing those little things each day, I practice on me. "Make sure you establish a great relationship with yourself, because you are the only you know for certain that you will always be with." Wilson Gunter. Okay one more quote from my grandfather that is spot on, "Son, treat everyone right, but don't you dare treat them the same." Wilson Gunter. We all have a story so, take the time to not only listen to someone's story but, actually hear what they are saying. We are indeed more alike than we are different.

6. Be open to learning: Stay open to learning new things throughout your life. Seek out new experiences, perspectives, and knowledge. This will help you grow and evolve as a person and will enhance your ability to make a lasting impact. There is nothing more satisfying or rewarding than learning something new. Every new thing learned is an opportunity to be something or grow into something that's better than what you were a day, hour, minute, or second before. I wear my nerd badge proudly. Without being willing to be open to the possibilities of what knowledge could bring into my life I would not be who I am today. We all get dealt a certain hand in life and no matter how good or bad that had is, your willingness to learn can make all of the difference in the world. Life ebbs and flows and you can start with a lot and end up with a little or nothing or you can start with nothing and end up with a lot or everything. It boils down to listening well, understanding what you heard, and applying yourself. Yep, you will eventually have to do the work. Seek out new experiences because they more time than not create new opportunities and new perspectives. Old methods do not equal new results. You will never have a revolution of knowledge in your life if you are not willing to evolve. On my podcast Almon Gunter Experience I talk about the revolution being real. The revolution that I am talking about is information. Information is how we evolve. It's how we grow and truly create progress and change. "There is no such thing as a peaceful revolution." Malcolm X. Commit to learning for life.

Every day learn one new thing and then pass it on. Every r**EVOL**ution comes with love.

Remember, building a lasting legacy takes time and effort, but the impact you make will be worth it. By living a life guided by your values, setting clear goals, taking action, sharing your knowledge, building meaningful relationships, and staying open to learning, you can leave a positive and lasting legacy. Spend each day building something that will last long after you are physically here.

A story of a lasting legacy:

Jesus, Buddha, Muhammad, Vishnu, The Great Spirit, Kemet, Mansa Musa, Queen Nefertiti, Queen Amina of Zaria, Harriet Tubman, WEB Dubois, Mother Teresa, Frederick Douglas, Sojourner Truth, Malcolm X, Dr. Martin Luther King Jr, Fannie Lou Hamer, Aristotle, Carter G Woodson, Katherine Johnson, Dorothy Vaughan, Mary Jackson, Muhammad Ali, Zeus, Steve Jobs, Henry Dunant, Dr. David b Langston, Dr. Dennis B Webber, Eunice and Almon W Gunter Sr., Wilson Gunter,

...

Scribbles and Doodles

What are some of the values you have that play a major role in who you are and what your legacy will be?

____

____

____

____

____

____

____

____

____

List a few goals you are currently pursuing and the methods you are using to measure your success of each goal?

____

____

____

____

____

____

____

____

____

What things do you do each day to ensure that you continue to be a lifelong learner? And how will those things ensure a lasting legacy?

____

____

____

____

____

____

____

____

____

Final Thoughts:

____

____

____

____

____

____

____

____

____

____

SUMMARY

Mentoring is a powerful tool for creating a lasting legacy. Mentoring is a process where an experienced individual guides and supports a less experienced individual in their personal and professional growth. By sharing their knowledge and expertise, mentors can help mentees avoid common pitfalls and achieve their goals faster. The impact of mentoring can last a lifetime, as the skills and insights gained can be applied in various areas of life. Effective mentoring can leave a lasting legacy that extends beyond the mentor-mentee relationship.

To create a lasting legacy through mentoring, it is important to approach the process with intentionality. Mentors should have clear goals for the relationship, and a plan for achieving those goals. They should also be open and honest with their mentee about their own experiences and challenges, and encourage their mentee to be honest and transparent as well. By building a strong foundation of trust and mutual respect, mentors can create a lasting legacy that goes beyond the immediate benefits of the mentoring relationship.

One key to creating a lasting legacy through mentoring is to focus on helping the mentee develop their own leadership skills. Mentors should encourage their mentee to take ownership of their own growth and development, and provide guidance and support as needed. This approach can help the mentee build confidence and develop the skills they need to lead others in the future. By investing in the development of the mentee's leadership skills, the mentor can create a lasting legacy that extends beyond their own contributions.

Finally, to create a lasting legacy through mentoring, it is important to stay connected with the mentee over time. Mentors should maintain an ongoing relationship with their mentee, providing support and guidance as needed. By staying connected, mentors can continue to have a positive impact on their mentee's personal and professional growth, and can create a lasting legacy that extends well beyond the initial mentoring relationship.

Final Thoughts:

About the Author

Motivation, Noun. def. To provide with motive.

Motive, Noun. Def. Something that causes a person to act. A stimulus to action. Motive implies an emotion or desire operating on the will and causing it to act.

While Merriam-Webster gives us these definitions in words, Almon Gunter gives us these definitions in actions. Almon shares his desire for all individuals to possess the motivation, dedication, and determination to succeed in achieving their goals. His formula for success involves steadfast dedication, never-ending enthusiasm, hard work, heart and hustle, with the end result of becoming a MVP in the game of life.

Almon Gunter is the CEO/President of AGE 3, LLC. He is a highly acclaimed motivational, inspirational public speaker, author, and consultant, as well as a world-class sprinter in US Track and Field. He uses his past experiences on the track to help inspire others in the game of life.

Almon Gunter is a life coach that focuses on mental and physical fitness. He believes that all people have goals and asks them what their goals are from day one. He believes that every individual can achieve anything they set their mind on and helps them believe that the tools for achieving these goals are within themselves. His role is to help all individuals find their inner tools and refine them into razor-sharp instruments. Once these tools are refined, individuals who learn and follow Almon's encouraging words will build self-confidence that will benefit them in their chosen fields.

Acknowledgments

Special thanks to Beverly (Bevy) for your encouragement and support in everything I do. You always seem to know what I need and when I need it most. I hope we continue to laugh every day and make each other 1% better each day. To my kids, keep writing your own stories. Embrace adversity, because everything you desire is just on the other side of having the courage to go through it. The greatest growth comes from the hardest struggle.

Shout out to my dear friend David Hodges for agreeing to write the forward to this book. I really appreciate you and I am so blessed to know you and have you as a friend and a brother. Keep fighting the good fight.

Thanks to my best friends from the short pants days Windle (Peck) and Earriet (Easy) for always being on my team. Also, thank you to Ricky Battle and Tommy Sampson for always finding the time to check in and say hello; you two are such great friends. To my brothers and sisters who grew up in the same house but different addresses, Carl Tremble, Bruce Canady, Greg Dorsey, Tracy Maxwell, Joel Fouraker, Cassandra Jenkins, and Connie Jenkins-Pye.

Thanks to all of my mentors and coaches who have pushed, encouraged, and prayed for me along the way, especially coaches Claude Simmons, Larry Monts, and Andrea Bowman. There are so many others that helped me along the way, and I say thank you. Please know that my journey is not complete so keep encouraging, embracing, and challenging me to do even greater things. Each of us have the power within us to get 1% better each day! If we learn one new thing every day, we can then teach one new thing every day. Whatever you want to see in the world, must first start with you. Lead, serve, teach, coach, mentor. Every day is game day!

Gunter out!

For more information
On other products by
Almon W. Gunter, Jr.

KEYNOTE
BOOKS
TRAINING CAMPS
CONSULTING

Please Contact:

Almon Gunter Experience, LLC
Post Office Box 194
Jacksonville, FL32234
Office Phone: 904.803.1917

Website: www.almongunterexperience.com

Via-email: almon@almongunterexperience.com

Twitter: @almongunter

Facebook: Almon W Gunter Jr

Linkedin: Almon Gunter

Give AGE 3, LLC a call today to start your
transformation!
#Everydayisgameday